The Blue Corn Cookbook

by
Celine-Marie Pascale

Out West Publishing • Albuquerque, NM

Y ou got no business cooking if you don't feel right. If you can't stop yourself from being mad or sad or tired or something, don't cook for other people. The old folks used to tell us to always be thinking something good, especially when you're doing something for somebody else.

Hattie Harjo, Chickasaw elder

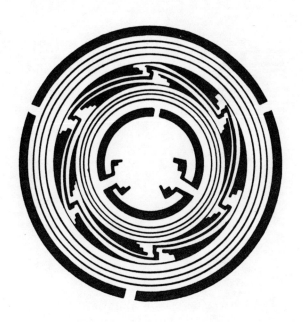

Y ou get the strangest cooking a poor life, right. If
you can't stop you will from being told or told to
tired of something that it won't for other people.
The old arts used well as to thinks be thinking
is nothing good, especially when you're doing something
for somebody else.

Contents

Preface

Before cooking became a science or an art, it was a way of prayer, a way of healing. Pueblo people believe that the thoughts, feelings, and prayers of the cook are passed along through the food. Pueblo women have prepared ceremonial food for centuries; they will tell you that your intention when you cook is as important as any recipe.

In the warmth of their homes and by the work of their hands, Pueblo women have passed recipes through generations. Without a written language, they had no recipe books, no weights or measures. Had we each been born into Native American homes, we would have learned to cook gradually and continually. We would have also learned the legends and traditions surrounding the food we ate and the way we lived. We would each have known from the time that we were very small, that it is a great gift to be fed and an inexpressible honor to feed another person.

Pueblo women, historically, have had a talent for creating simple, nutritious foods that can be prepared quickly and with great variation. Traditional recipes depended on resources that were different from what we have available now. For instance, powdered fruit was the primary sweetener in recipes, and animal fat was used instead of butter, margarine, or oil. I have had the great honor of being able to include some traditional recipes in this collection. These recipes have been adapted to modern resources, but the spirit is the same in that each traditional recipe can be prepared as simply or as elaborately as time and resources allow. All of these recipes can be enjoyed hot or cold.

This collection also includes recipes created by me and other non-Indian women. I have been concerned about my ability to share my experience with blue corn without compromising or misrepresenting Native American cultures. My intention is to provide a wide spectrum of possibilities for cooking with blue corn, and, at the same time, to retain the distinction and integrity of Native American traditions.

I would like to thank all of the Left Hand family, Grandma Santanita in particular, for her kindness and for the traditional recipes she was able to contribute to this collection. I first learned about blue corn from her son, Richard Romero (Deertrack), whom I met in 1981. Richard and I shared the belief that it is possible for Native Peoples to achieve economic stability through traditional technologies - such as organic farming and

consequently formed the Blue Corn Trading Company to package and distribute traditionally grown blue corn.

Many of the traditional recipes included here belong to his family. I am grateful to Robert Romero, Richard's son, for his friendship, kindness, and humor. I also want to thank Robert's great-grandmother, Hattie Harjo, for her friendship and encouragement.

I left the Blue Corn Trading Company in 1985 and, with Barbara Marden, opened a blue corn breakfast restaurant, The Red Willow. At heart, however, I am a writer and poet, not a restaurateur. I left the restaurant that same year to return to writing, developing recipes, and teaching cooking workshops.

Both the Red Willow and the Blue Corn Trading Company used wonderful recipes created by Jeanne Vaughn, and many of her recipes are included here as well. I especially want to thank Jeanne for her generous and adventurous nature. She also provided a sense of camaraderie that inspired many of my own recipes. Many thanks go to Dinah Drago, Kate Henke, Haydée Frederickson, and Terry Sever who each shared recipes with me. I also want to thank Tana Santa Cruz for her helpful suggestions. I'm grateful to Pete Shanks for his generous support in all phases of this project. Many thanks to the folks at Out West Publishing, in particular Robert Spiegel and Lois Bergthold for their care and thoughtfulness.

To my mother belong deepest thanks and prayers. From her I learned to love cooking and, as importantly, to rebel against the daily expectations that can turn love into tyranny.

I hope the recipes and lives represented in this book bring you enjoyment and help you to find your own place among the traditional and the modern.

Introduction
Blue Corn . . . The Beginning

Taos Pueblo Elders say that at the beginning of Time, when all of the People were gathered together preparing to walk upon Mother Earth, the Creator spoke to them and gave them four kinds of corn: blue, yellow, red, and white. The Creator told the People that they would be the caretakers of corn and taught them how to plant and harvest and how to use corn for food, medicine, and prayer.

Each type of corn is associated with one of the four directions. Yellow Corn is associated with the South, the home of the grandmothers and grandfathers who bring us Spring and new life. Red Corn belongs to the West, the direction the sun travels. They say that our spirits travel westward when we cross over; the West is the place that gives us long life. To the North is White Corn and the grandmothers and grandfathers who bring us strength. Blue Corn is related to the East, the place of the rising sun, the direction that brings wisdom and understanding. When children are born, blue corn is used in their naming. As they grow, they rely upon blue corn in prayer and in healing. And when they are called home, it is blue corn that their loved ones bury with them.

The People were taught how to respect corn and how to care for it. Corn cannot seed itself. If an ear falls off of the stalk, it will rot before the kernels can germinate. Corn must be husked, shelled, and planted.

Through the silence of heavy snows, the traditional adobe ovens at Taos Pueblo stand sentinel; they witness the changing of days and anchor an entire civilization to a history and a future. Built by family, friends, and neighbors, each oven has a history, a life, and a lineage. Wide and low to the ground, the ovens look like bee hives. Smoke holes and doorways are charred with age and use. The door is a simple board braced against the oven with a rock.

In the evening, sticks of piñon and juniper are stacked in the belly of the oven. In the morning when the air is cool, the fire is lit. As it burns, the smoke hole is opened to increase ventilation, and jagged cracks in the outer adobe wall are mended with mud.

In a few hours when the wood is reduced to ash and coal, the door is opened and the smoke hole closed. All of the coals and ash are carefully raked out to make room for bread and pies.

Like bees to a hive, children and grandchildren carry loaves of bread to the women who tend the oven. The ovens are large; more than twenty loaves bake at one time.

The women lift loaves of newly risen bread out of the pans and onto long-handled peels and then slide them onto the oven floor without ever disturbing the dough. When the bread is done, children carry the hot loaves of bread back to the kitchen where the women rub each loaf with lard and stack them to cool. A modern gas stove among loaves of bread testifies to the passage of time and the strength of tradition.

From an Obsessed Cook

In 1980 I was invited to prepare blue corn cereal for a religious ceremony Richard Romero was conducting. I had seen many women prepare exactly the same recipe and produce amazingly different results. I was no different and found out then just how important my attitude and intention could be in the kitchen. I have been exploring the uncharted possibilities of cooking with blue corn since.

Most of the recipes I have created came to me in dreams over a period of years. On many occasions, I have awakened flinging off covers in search of eggs, only to find that when fully awake, I had the complete details of a new recipe. These "instant" discoveries led me to explore and develop more recipes.

Blue Corn provides one of the most magical adventures in cooking imaginable. I made some discoveries by chance-as when I forgot to bake a cake I had made. By evening, when I found it outside, the batter had become a brilliant turquoise color; it was delicious! Other discoveries were inspired by necessity or abundance. I've included some of the discoveries I've made on my way to creating recipes. Perhaps these will help you to create your own.

If you have whole kernel blue corn and want to grind it yourself, it is important to know whether you have raw or roasted kernels. Only roasted kernels have a golden brown coloration. Raw whole kernel corn can be roasted in a cast iron frying pan over a medium heat until golden brown. To avoid scorching, the corn must be stirred constantly. Allow the corn to cool slightly before grinding.

If you purchased roasted whole kernels, heat them in an oven (350°) for fifteen minutes or so to warm them before grinding. Warm corn is much easier to grind by home-style methods. To grind the corn you will need either a good flour mill (on the finest setting) or grinding stones.

Blue cornmeal which has not been roasted will leave a "green," bitter taste and will require more cooking. In some recipes this can go unnoticed, either because the dish is baked, or because the strength of the other ingredients masks the subtleties. I prefer roasted blue corn for all recipes; there are, however, a few for which it is essential. Roasting brings out the richest possible flavor of the corn.

When you purchase blue cornmeal, taste a bit of your blue corn before cooking. If it has been roasted, it will have a nutty flavor. If your cornmeal has not been roasted, you can toast it yourself in a cast iron frying pan over medium heat. Stir constantly and remove the blue corn from the pan as soon as it turns golden. This will provide a wonderful flavor; however, it will also destroy some of the nutrition. For this reason I recommend that you purchase only roasted blue cornmeal. It has been slowly heated before being ground and retains more nutritional value.

Despite the hard outer shell of the kernel of the blue corn, the inner flesh is actually softer than other varieties of corn. Consequently, it produces the soft look of flour rather that the coarse texture you would expect in a cornmeal. Finely ground blue corn can be used in almost any recipe. Unlike wheat flour, it does not have gluten and, therefore, produces light, moist, textures most easily when blended with other flours. Half blue corn and half unbleached white flour is a successful combination. The proportions can be varied to create the desired texture and color. The nutritional advantage of using whole wheat flour with blue corn is offset by the grainy, dense texture it creates. I have experimented with oat flour, which is a wonderful complement to blue corn and makes both a nutritional and aesthetic contribution to the meal.

Blue corn reacts to the amount and type of fat used in the recipe. Heavier oils such as butter tend to produce deeper colors, usually a soft purple. Light oil such as safflower will create shades that tend toward blue-green. The intensity of any shade depends upon how long the batter stands before it is cooked. Because blue corn reacts to fat, the type of milk that is used will also change the color of the corn. Non-fat and instant milk usually turn the corn to cement grey.

Using honey in place of sugar creates a dense, heavy color. The exact shade depends on the type of honey used. Most honeys tend to produce purples. Since honey can overwhelm the subtle flavor of the corn, use it sparingly. I don't recommend using honey and non-fat milk together; the combination masks the delicate flavor and color of the blue corn.

Even the cookware can affect the color of the corn. Cast iron can produce magnificent purples. When cooking in cast iron, add just a small amount of butter to the batter or use a lighter oil (for muffins, etc.). Aluminum, which generally is harmful because it contaminates food, brings out the blue-green side of the corn, while stainless steel tends toward a lovely periwinkle. Sometimes the smallest things can change the texture or color. There aren't any rules to memorize; it helps to develop a relationship with the corn, a "feel for it."

Notes on Ingredients

Blue Corn

I used this term instead of cornmeal to avoid the granular connotations of a coarse, heavy meal. The blue corn used in most of these recipes is much closer to the consistency of flour. Use coarsely ground blue corn only where noted.

Blue corn traditionally grown on Native American lands is one of the purest foods in existence today. It has never been hybridized, and it has never been sprayed or fertilized with chemicals of any kind. Blue corn grown by traditional ways is nurtured by clear mountain water which still runs freely through the high country.

There are a few agribusinesses that grow blue corn. It is less expensive than traditionally grown blue corn but the money saved costs us something priceless. Please support Native Americans and their traditionally grown blue corn.

Flour

All flours were not created equal. I prefer to use unbleached white flour or oat flour in all of these recipes. You can use bleached white, whole wheat, or whole wheat pastry flour. Do not substitute rice flour. It might be profitable to make notations in the margins of the book as you go. Flours require different amounts of liquid and will, of course, yield different results.

Chiles

Use New Mexican (formerly, "Anaheim"), unless noted. Fresh, frozen, or canned may each be used according to preference.

Chile Powder

I use only plain and pure New Mexico chile powder because I love the flavor and the fire. If you don't have a preference of your own, try experimenting with pure chile powders (not those mixed with herbs and spices). The results will be surprising.

CHAPTER ONE

From the Source: Native American Traditional Recipes

BLUE CORN CEREAL

This cereal is delicious with the addition of nuts and dried fruit or a dash of cinnamon or nutmeg. If the cereal is allowed to cook for fifteen minutes, it will gel into a wonderful pudding when it cools. It may be necessary to add small amounts of water to the cereal to keep it cooking for fifteen minutes without sticking.

>2 cups roasted blue corn, finely ground
>2 cups cold water
>2 cups boiling water
>1/2 teaspoon salt
>butter and sweetener to taste

Coarse and fine grinds of blue corn will yield diverse, though equally delicious results. Mix blue corn with cold water. Add salt to the water and being to a full boil. Stir blue corn and water briskly; then quickly and carefully, add it to the boiling water stirring with a whisk (as you pour) to prevent lumping. Cook until cereal thickens (about five minutes), stirring frequently. Add butter and sweetener just before serving.

Serves six.

AGAINST-THE-FIRE

The griddle cakes are especially good slathered with butter and chokecherry jam.

     2 cups blue corn, finely ground
     1 cup flour
     1 Tablespoon baking powder
     warm water

Combine the dry ingredients and cut-in butter as for biscuits. Slowly add warm water to make a soft, but not sticky dough. Allow to stand for a few minutes. The blue corn will absorb the moisture and become slightly dry. Now add more water to keep a soft, smooth texture.

Break off balls about 3 inches in diameter and roll out on a well-floured surface to 1/4 inch thickness. Cook on a hot, dry griddle as for tortillas.

This makes about eight very hearty servings.

INDIAN BANANAS

Traditionally prepared as backpacking food to be carried into the high country, Indian Bananas are tough, chewy, nutritious, and hearty. They make an excellent snack for the children.

> 2 cups roasted blue corn, fine to medium grind
> honey or sugar to taste (just a dollop)
> warm water
> raisins or other dried fruit
> pecans
> cornhusks

Soak the cornhusks in a bowl of warm water to soften. Combine blue corn with a handful or two of dried fruit and nuts. Dissolve the honey in a little warm water (if sugar is preferred, add it to the dry blue corn). Slowly add the warm water to the blue corn until it forms a thick soft dough which neither crumbles nor sticks to the hands.

Select a half dozen cornhusks which are thick, yet pliable, and dry them off. Shape the batter in the palm of your hand making it about 1/4 inch thick and about 2" x 3" in size. Place this into the center of the cornhusk and wrap husk around it. Fold the edges of the corn husk as if wrapping a package, then tie it shut with a piece of string or cornhusk.

The "bananas" can now be baked in the oven at 350° or around the coals of a campfire. Cook about one hour until the cornhusk is golden and slightly brittle. The middle will be firm—the firmer, the better. Peel and eat warm or cold.

Depending on the size of the cornhusk, the types and amount of goodies added, and the amount of filling used, this recipe will make about a dozen "bananas."

BROWN BETTY
(Little Sister)

Little Sister is sweet and tough as nails. More sugar as well as dried fruits or nuts can be added, according to personal preference. Chewy and nutritious, it makes an excellent backpacking food.

> 2 cups roasted blue corn, finely ground
> 1 cup whole wheat flour
> 1/4 cup sugar
> 1 2/3 cups water (warm to hot)

In a heavy pan, melt the sugar into a brown syrup. Carefully add a small portion of water to it. The syrup will spit. Stir until smooth and continue adding water until the two are combined; turn off heat. In another bowl, mix the flour and blue corn together. Add the sugar water to the dry ingredients and mix well. Pour into a greased 8" x 8" pan and swirl the top of the batter to create a textured surface. Bake for one hour at 350°. The bread will turn golden brown and will be hard as leather.

Makes about a dozen bars.

FRYING PAN BREAD

The nutty, rich flavor of blue corn mellows this sweet spicy cornbread.

> 1 1/2 cups wheat flour
> 1 1/2 cups blue corn, fine to medium grind
> 2 Tablespoons baking powder
> 1 teaspoon salt
> 1/4 cup sugar
> 2 Tablespoons grated jack or cheddar cheese
> 1/4 cup sweet green pepper, chopped
> 1/4 onion, chopped
> 2 Tablespoons shortening
> 4 teaspoons chile powder
> 1 1/2 cup milk
> 2 eggs, lightly beaten

Mix the dry ingredients together-except the chile powder. Melt the shortening in a large cast iron skillet, add the chile powder and cool. This skillet will become the baking pan. Add the shortening and chile mixture to the dry ingredients, then fold in the cheese, onion, and peppers. In a measuring cup or separate bowl, blend the milk and eggs before adding them to the dry ingredients. Stir well and return to the large skillet used for melting the shortening. Don't clean the skillet before pouring in the batter. Bake for 35 minutes at 400°.

Yields about a dozen hearty servings.

PINOLE
(Hot Corn Drink)

This extraordinary beverage tastes like a cross between cocoa and hot custard!

> 2 cups roasted blue corn, finely ground
> 1/2 cup sugar
> 1 teaspoon cinnamon
> Milk

The blue corn must be very finely ground and roasted for this recipe. Combine sugar, cinnamon, and blue corn. Use approximately one Tablespoon per cup of milk. Allow the corn and milk mixture to simmer for ten minutes over low heat until it thickens slightly, stirring frequently.

BLUE CORN DUMPLINGS

Add these dumplings to soups or stews fifteen minutes before serving. The dumplings will thicken any broth.

> 2 cups roasted blue corn, finely ground
> 2 teaspoons baking powder
> 1 teaspoon salt
> 1/4 cup shortening
> 3/4 cup milk

Combine the dry ingredients. Cut in the shortening. Add milk until the dough becomes moist enough to mold. Shape the dough into oblong dumplings, not more than one inch thick and two inches long.

Makes about one dozen.

BLUE CORN POLENTA

This is a wonderful, hearty breakfast food that has also been known to show up in place of rice on dinner plates.

>   1 cup blue corn, coarsely ground
>   2 cups water, lightly salted

Add the blue corn to the boiling water. Stir enthusiastically and cook until soft and thick. (If the blue corn is not a coarse grind, it will lump disastrously). Serve it with butter and garlic, or with honey or syrup.

Serves four.

CHACKEWE
(Atole)

Unlike the creamy decadence of Pinole, Chackewe is a thin, grainy beverage with a rich and simple flavor. It's ideal for fasting or convalescing.

> 1 cup roasted blue corn, finely ground
> 1 quart boiling water
> salt and sweetener to taste

Mix blue corn with a little cold water until it is soupy. This mixing will help to prevent lumping. Add the mixture to the boiling water and cook for a few minutes, until it thickens a little. Add a little cinnamon or milk, if desired.
Makes four servings.

TORTILLAS

Pueblo traditions require, as a matter of respect for the tortilla, that once a tortilla is removed from the griddle, it always rests "face" up. The last side of the tortilla to touch the griddle is called the face of the tortilla. You will be able to recognize it with very little practice.

Nearly 1/2" thick, these are soft, bread-like tortillas, not at all like the tortillas sold in stores.

> 1 cup roasted blue corn, finely ground
> 1 cup unbleached white flour
> 2 Tablespoons butter
> 1 Tablespoon baking powder
> hot water

Combine all dry ingredients. Cut in the butter. Gradually add very hot water until a soft, but not a sticky, dough is made. Knead well and allow to rest for ten minutes. Break off a medium size ball and roll (press or pat) into a tortilla 1/4" thick. Bake on an ungreased (but well seasoned) griddle until lightly browned. When the bottom is lightly brown and the raw side is puffy, gently turn the tortilla over.

Makes about 6 tortillas.

NAVAJO CAKE

This is a sweet, dense bread with a rich flavor. Because Navajo Cake is cooked slowly in a low heat, it is easy to make over a campfire, once a good bed of coals has been established. To do this, use a large frying pan and a lid instead of a 9" x 13" pan and foil.

> 2 cups boiling water
> 4 cups cooked blue corn cereal (see page 15)
> 2 cups cooked yellow cornmeal
> 1 cup sprouted wheat
> 1/2 cup raisins
> 1/2 cup brown sugar

Mix all of the ingredients together and pour into a 9" x 13" pan, cover with foil, and bake for four hours at 250°.

Cut into 18 portions.

CHAPTER TWO
Breakfasts

BLUE CORN PANCAKES

Add currants, raisins, poppyseeds, or nuts to the batter for an additional change of pace.

> 1 cup roasted blue corn, finely ground
> 1 cup whole wheat pastry flour (or unbleached white)
> 1 Tablespoon baking powder
> 1/4 teaspoon salt
> 1 Tablespoon sugar
> 2 eggs, beaten
> 1 cup milk
> 1/4 cup melted butter

Combine the dry ingredients in one bowl and the wet ingredients in another. Slowly add wet ingredients to the dry, being sure to eliminate lumps. Fry on a griddle as for regular pancakes. Makes about a dozen pancakes.

JEANNE'S BLUE CORN COTTAGE CHEESE PANCAKES

Jeanne's talent for refined simplicity reached a pinnacle with this recipe. These crepe-like pancakes are wonderful with syrup or filled with fresh fruit and whipped cream. After making this recipe once, cooks will undoubtedly want to double it. It keeps well for several days in the fridge. These pancakes are light and tasty. The trick is in frying them. They demand a well-greased griddle over moderate heat and patience. If you try to turn them too soon, you'll make a mess.

> 2-3 eggs, depending on size
> 2 Tablespoons butter
> 1/4 cup roasted blue corn, finely ground
> a pinch of salt
> 1 cup cottage cheese

Mix eggs, butter, salt, and cottage cheese together. Slowly add blue corn, stirring slowly. Using a well-greased skillet, pour batter into skillet. Wait for the spatula to slide easily under the whole pancake before turning. If the griddle was greased with a lot of butter, the pancake may be very dark when it is turned. The pancake will be okay, but use less butter on the next one.

Makes 6 pancakes.

BLUE CORN WAFFLES

After creating this recipe, I then proved that it is possible to live for an extended period of time by eating only waffles.

> 1 1/2 cups roasted blue corn, finely ground
> 1 1/2 cups oat flour or unbleached white
> 1 Tablespoon baking powder
> 1/2 teaspoon salt*
> 1 Tablespoon brown sugar
> 3 eggs, beaten lightly
> 1 1/4 cups milk
> 1/2 cup sweet butter
> 1/4 cup walnuts finely chopped (opt.)
> *Note: If you need to use salted butter, omit salt
> from the recipe.

Melt the butter. In a large bowl combine all dry ingredients and mix well. Combine the eggs and milk and add to the dry ingredients. Stir in the melted butter. As the batter stands, it will continue to thicken, so more milk may be needed, particularly if oat flour is used. The batter should be thicker than the pancake batter, but not stiff. Bake in a hot, greased waffle iron until done.

Makes 8 waffles.

HONEY-NUT CAKE

This is a delicious version of sticky-buns "right-side up."

The Cake:
1 cup roasted blue corn, finely ground
1 cup unbleached white flour
2 teaspoons baking powder
1/2 cup butter
1 cup milk
1 egg
1 teaspoon vanilla

The Glaze:
1/4 cup butter
1/2 cup honey
2 cups walnuts, chopped
1 egg white

Mix all dry ingredients together. Cut-in the butter as for biscuits and then add the milk, egg, and vanilla. Stir well. Pour into a well-greased 10" spring pan and immediately put into the freezer while preparing the glaze.

Preheat the oven to 350° and begin the glaze. In a medium sauce pan, melt the butter and honey together. When the butter and honey are well-blended and cooled slightly, add the egg white and mix well. Add the nuts and mix. Remove the cake from the freezer, cover it with the glaze, and slide it into the oven for 20-30 minutes.

Serves twelve.

BLUE CORN CINNAMON ROLLS

Cinnamon rolls are among my favorite foods, so I was particularly eager to create a blue corn cinnamon roll. Unfortunately, it is nearly impossible to use blue corn in a yeasted dough. Jeanne created a cinnamon roll based on a variation of a biscuit recipe, and for months we made every sort of cinnamon roll we could imagine using a baking powder batter. This is my favorite.

The Dough:
1 cup roasted blue corn, finely ground
1 cup unbleached white flour
1 Tablespoon baking powder
1/2 teaspoon salt
1/2 cup butter
1/2 cup milk
2 eggs

The Filling:
1 cup brown sugar or date sugar
2 Tablespoons cinnamon and/or cocoa
1/2 cup finely chopped walnuts or almonds

Combine the dry ingredients and mix well. Cut in the butter. In a separate bowl or measuring cup, combine the milk and eggs. Add the wet ingredients to the dry ingredients. Mix well. On a lightly floured surface, roll dough into a rectangle 1/2" thick. Cover with sugar, cinnamon, and/or cocoa. Sprinkle with chopped nuts. Roll up the dough from the widest edge, keeping the turns tight. Pinch ends closed. With a sharp knife, slice into rolls two-fingers wide. Place on an ungreased cookie sheet and bake at 425° for 10 minutes, until golden.

Makes one dozen.

TERRY'S DATE-NUT BREAD

Who would have thought three bananas would equal one cup of sugar? Terry Sever is the kind of woman who will figure these things out. It's a great way to reduce the amount of refined sugar. Over-ripe bananas can be stored in the freezer indefinitely.

This is a variation of a date-nut bread Terry makes and a great example of how to improvise on recipes. This recipe is the same as Terry's original, except that I've altered the amount and types of flour. By now I've made so many versions that I don't remember what kind of flour the original recipe used.

> 1 pound (2 cups) pitted, chopped dates
> 1 1/2 cups boiling water
> 1 cup sugar or 1/2 cup honey or 3 ripe bananas
> 1 1/2 Tablespoons butter
> 2 eggs
> 1 teaspoon vanilla
> 1 cup roasted blue corn, finely ground
> 1 3/4 cups flour
> 2 teaspoons baking powder
> 1/2 teaspoon salt
> 1 cup chopped walnuts

Preheat the oven to 350° and grease a bundt pan or two small loaf pans. Pour boiling water over the dates and let them stand. In a separate bowl, cream the butter, sugar, vanilla, and eggs. Add the liquid from the dates. Then add the baking powder, salt, blue corn, and flour. Mix well. Add the dates and nuts last. Pour into pan(s) and bake about one hour.

Makes about twelve servings.

BLUEBERRY MUFFINS

Blueberries are a natural complement to any blue corn dish. Unbleached white or whole wheat flour may be used in this recipe.

> 1 cup roasted blue corn, finely ground
> 1 cup flour
> 1/2 teaspoon salt
> 1 Tablespoon baking powder
> 1/2 cup brown sugar
> 4 Tablespoons butter
> 2 eggs
> 1 cup milk
> 1/2 cup blueberries

Preheat oven to 400°. Grease 16 muffin cups. To avoid over-mixing, use two bowls; in one, combine all the dry ingredients, in the other, all the wet ingredients (creaming butter and sugar together first). Add the wet ingredients to the dry ingredients, mixing evenly but not stirring hard. Pour into greased muffin pans and bake for 15 or 20 minutes. Be sure each muffin cup is only 2/3 full, or the muffin mixture will overflow.

Makes 16 muffins.

BLUE CORN COFFEE CAKE

This recipe rivals my love for chocolate-filled croissants, but then, I'm in favor of anything that justifies chocolate for breakfast.

The Cake:
1/2 cup sugar
1/2 cup sweet butter
2 eggs
1 cup sour cream
1 teaspoon vanilla
1 cup roasted blue corn, finely ground
1 cup unbleached white flour
1 teaspoon baking powder
1/2 teaspoon baking soda
1/4 teaspoon salt

The Filling:
4 ounces unsweetened chocolate, grated
3/4 cup chopped walnuts
1/4 cup sugar

Preheat the oven to 350°. Prepare the filling by combining the ingredients and set aside. Then sift the blue corn, flour, baking powder, baking soda, and salt together. In a separate bowl cream the butter, sugar, eggs, vanilla, and sour cream. Slowly add the dry ingredients to the wet and mix well.

Pour 1/2 of the batter into a well-greased 10" spring pan. Sprinkle 1/2 of the filling over the batter. Add the remaining batter and top with last half of filling. Bake for 30-35 minutes at 350°.

Serves twelve.

CHAPTER THREE

Appetizers

CHINESE-STYLE DUMPLINGS

The soft, doughy texture of the blue corn roulade on 47 reminded me of the Chinese pot stickers I enjoy so much and eventually led to this recipe.

The Dumplings:
5 small-medium potatoes
1 egg
1 cup roasted blue corn, finely ground
1/4 teaspoon salt

Boil the potatoes until nearly done. After they cool enough to be handled, peel and grate them. Add the egg and salt to the potatoes. Stir well and then slowly add the blue corn. The goal is to make a dough that can be easily handled.

The Filling:
1/4 cup cilantro, chopped
1/2 cup parsley, chopped
1 bunch scallions, minced
3 cloves garlic, crushed
cayenne pepper, soy sauce, and sesame oil to taste
1/2 pound ground meat (beef, chicken or pork)

Brown the meat with the garlic. Add the cilantro, parsley, and scallions, and simmer. Add cayenne pepper, soy sauce, and sesame oil to taste. Spread the dumpling dough (no more than 1/4 inch thick) across your palm. Add a Tablespoon or so of filling. Gently close your palm and pinch the edges of the dumpling closed. Shape the dumpling into a crescent at this point. Place each one into a steaming basket as it is made. I recommend steaming a test dumpling to be sure the water is not too deep and to give a better idea of how they will look when done. If these are over-cooked, they are very mushy. Check on the dumplings after 5 minutes, but expect to give them about 8 minutes.

These are great when dipped into a bit of soy sauce and can be an appetizer or side dish.

Makes about 10 dumplings.

SHRIMP COCKTAIL

Just when it seemed that parties were doomed to the standard shrimp cocktail sauce, this recipe was created. This sauce is more than just spicy. It's equally good warm or cold and combines a complex flavor with a kick.

> 1 cup water
> 1/2 cup blue corn, finely ground
> 2 cloves garlic
> 2 teaspoons horseradish
> 1 teaspoon Dijon mustard
> 1/2 teaspoon cayenne powder (more or less to taste)
> 1 teaspoon mayonnaise
> 2 dozen poached shrimp

Combine the blue corn and water in a small sauce pan. Cook over medium heat and stir for five minutes. It will bubble and thicken and probably spit, and that indicates when to turn if off. Add the crushed garlic, horseradish, mustard, mayonnaise, and cayenne. Stir well and let sit a while before adding more cayenne. This makes 1 cup of the wildest lavender-pink dipping sauce.

Serves four.

STUFFED MUSHROOMS

One Saturday afternoon, I made something delicious but didn't have any idea what it was. Luckily, my friend Tana stopped over, took one taste and said, "What a great mushroom stuffing!" She was right.

    1 cup walnuts, finely ground
    1 cup sharp white cheddar, grated
    1/2 teaspoon thyme
    1/4 teaspoon marjoram
    1 onion, diced
    2 eggs
    1/2 cup well-toasted blue corn, finely ground
    grated parmesan cheese
    2 dozen large mushroom caps

Sauté the onion and spices. Combine the ground walnuts, cheddar cheese, and eggs. Mix well. Add the onion and spices. Stir in the blue corn to complete the filling. The filling can be prepared a day in advance.

Now prepare the mushrooms by washing them thoroughly and removing the stems. Lightly grease a cookie pan with butter. Fill mushroom caps with as much filling as they will hold and place them on the cookie sheet. Sprinkle the tops with parmesan cheese and broil for 5 minutes.

Serves six.

VEGETABLE DIP

For this recipe, the blue corn sold by the Blue Corn Trading Company and the roasted variety of blue corn sold by Casados Farms both work without additional fussing. This is as simple as it sounds. The blue corn adds a nutty flavor and texture to an otherwise creamy and lightly spicy dip.

1 cup cottage cheese
2 Tablespoons mayonnaise
1/4 teaspoon chile powder
1 clove garlic, crushed
2 Tablespoons roasted blue corn, finely ground

Combine the ingredients and mix well. Serve with sliced carrots, celery, cucumbers, or zucchini.

Makes one cup of dipping sauce.

CREAM CHEESE STICKS

This recipe demands that you think ahead; the advantage is that it keeps well for a day.

> 8 ounces cream cheese
> 4 ounces butter
> 1 clove garlic, crushed
> 1 cup roasted blue corn, finely ground
> 1 cup parmesan cheese, finely ground

Allow the cream cheese and butter to soften. Then cream them together. Add the garlic and blue corn. Mix well. On a lightly floured surface, roll the dough out to 1/2" thickness. Sprinkle generously with parmesan cheese; then fold the dough into thirds. Repeat this process twice more. Refrigerate the dough for one hour.

Preheat the oven to 375°. When the oven is ready, remove the dough from the refrigerator and roll out to 1/2" thickness. Cut into thin strips about 3/8" x 3" and place on an ungreased baking sheet. For an extra flair these can be twisted as they are placed onto the sheet. Bake for 10-15 minutes until they have brown bottoms and flaky tops.

Serves six.

CRAB PUFFS

Since these can be prepared a day in advance, they are an elegant and easy addition to any meal or party. The range in color, flavor, and temperature combine to make a dazzling appetizer.

The Filling:
3/4 cup cooked crab meat, shredded
1/2 teaspoon capers
1 teaspoon pimentos
1/4 teaspoon Coleman's Hot English Mustard
2 Tablespoons sour cream

The Pastry:
4 ounces cream cheese
2 ounces butter
1/2 cup roasted blue corn, finely ground

Allow the cream cheese and butter to soften; then cream together. Add blue corn and mix well. Roll out on a lightly floured board, fold into thirds, and roll out again. Repeat this process three times; then refrigerate the dough for 1 hour.

Combine the ingredients for the filling and mix well. Keep them refrigerated until used in the pastry.

Preheat oven to 375°. Use two cutters: one with a diameter of about 1 3/4" and another that will be small enough (about 1") to cut out the center of a circle.

When the dough is well-chilled, roll it out to 1/4" thickness. Use the 1 3/4" cutter to cut a circle of pastry; this will be a base. Cut another 1 3/4" circle and use the small cutter to remove the center from it. Place the O-shaped pastry on top of the base pastry (to create a well) and place it on an ungreased cookie sheet. Repeat.

Bake at 375° for 15 minutes. Immediately, after removing from the oven, fill the centers of each with a dollop of filling. Serve immediately. Makes one dozen.

CHAPTER FOUR

Entrées

BLUE CORN ROULADE

This recipe lends itself to being done in stages since both the spinach and potatoes are easiest to handle if cool. It's a very special meal that can be accomplished at a comfortable pace that allows the cook to revel in due praise.

The Filling:
2 pounds fresh spinach
2 Tablespoons butter
1 large onion, diced
1 large clove of garlic, crushed
2 Tablespoons sherry
3/4 teaspoon basil
1/4 teaspoon nutmeg
salt and pepper to taste

The Dough:
2 pounds potatoes broiled, peeled, and grated
3 eggs
1 cup roasted blue corn, finely ground
1 1/2 cups white flour
1 teaspoon salt
cheesecloth

The Garnish:
1/2 cup butter
grated parmesan cheese

Steam the spinach, allow it to cool, and then squeeze out all excess water. Dice and set aside. Sauté the butter, onion, and garlic. Add chopped spinach, sherry, and spices. Simmer for a few minutes, then allow to cool while preparing the dumpling.

Combine the grated potatoes with the eggs, salt, blue corn, and flour. Mix well. Roll out on a lightly floured board to be 11" x 14" x 1". Spread filling over the top, leaving about one inch clearance on the longest sides. Roll tightly and pat into a smooth, long roll. Wrap in several layers of cheesecloth to hold it together. Place in a baking pan 1/2 full of water and bake at 350° for 1 to 1 1/4 hours. Makes a rich, dumpling-like dough filled with spinach. To serve, slice, pour butter over it, and sprinkle with parmesan cheese.

Serves four to six.

BLUE CORN ROULADE

This recipe lends itself to being done in stages since both the spinach and potatoes are easiest to handle if cool. It's a very special meal that can be accomplished at a comfortable pace that allows the cook to revel in due praise.

The Filling:
2 pounds fresh spinach
2 Tablespoons butter
1 large onion, diced
1 large clove of garlic, crushed
2 Tablespoons sherry
3/4 teaspoon basil
1/4 teaspoon nutmeg
salt and pepper to taste

The Dough:
2 pounds potatoes broiled, peeled, and grated
3 eggs
1 cup roasted blue corn, finely ground
1 1/2 cups white flour
1 teaspoon salt
cheesecloth

The Garnish:
1/2 cup butter
grated parmesan cheese

Steam the spinach, allow it to cool, and then squeeze out all excess water. Dice and set aside. Sauté the butter, onion, and garlic. Add chopped spinach, sherry, and spices. Simmer for a few minutes, then allow to cool while preparing the dumpling.

Combine the grated potatoes with the eggs, salt, blue corn, and flour. Mix well. Roll out on a lightly floured board to be 11" x 14" x 1". Spread filling over the top, leaving about one inch clearance on the longest sides. Roll tightly and pat into a smooth, long roll. Wrap in several layers of cheesecloth to hold it together. Place in a baking pan 1/2 full of water and bake at 350° for 1 to 1 1/4 hours. Makes a rich, dumpling-like dough filled with spinach. To serve, slice, pour butter over it, and sprinkle with parmesan cheese.

Serves four to six.

PETE'S PASTICHE

The only thing more difficult than creating a recipe is naming one. This recipe was named after one of my many taste-testing friends. It's Pete's favorite recipe, or was, until he tried the ravioli.

These are excellent hot, cold, or straight from the fridge the next day. The filling can be made days in advance, but for best results, wait until the last minute to make the crust.

The filling:
1 onion, diced
1 bunch spinach
1/3 cup diced olives (optional)
salt & pepper to taste
1 cup cottage cheese
1 cup sharp cheddar cheese, grated
2 eggs

The Crust:
1 cup roasted blue corn, finely ground
1 cup white flour
1 Tablespoon baking powder
1/4 teaspoon salt
8 ounces cream cheese
2 eggs
1 egg yolk

Soften the cream cheese. Steam the spinach, squeeze out excess water, and dice. In a medium-size frying pan, sauté the onions, then add the chopped spinach, diced olives, salt and pepper. Mix well.

In a separate bowl, combine the cottage cheese, cheddar cheese, and eggs. Add the spinach and onion mixture and stir well. Set aside and begin the crust.

Combine the blue corn, white flour, baking powder, and salt. Mix well. Blend the cream cheese into the flour. Add the two eggs and work the dough (adding small amounts of flour as necessary) to a soft, but not sticky consistency.

Pinch off an egg-size ball and roll it out into a circle no more than 1/4 inch thick. Spread two Tablespoons of filling across the middle of the circle and fold the dough in half. Roll the edges toward the filling and crimp with fingers (as for pie crust) or with a fork to seal the edges. Prick the center several times with a fork. Repeat this process to make 8 turnovers.

Place pies on an ungreased baking sheet. Mix egg yolk with 2 Tablespoons cold water and brush over the pies just before baking. Bake 10-15 minutes at 400°. Most people will eat one turnover at a meal if it is served with other side dishes; more robust appetites will enjoy two.

Serves six.

CELI'S PASTICHE

If you're fond of gooey pizza, this is the pastiche for you; it has gobs of melted cheese securely sealed in a pouch. It's also a great way to use leftover spaghetti sauce.

The Crust:
1 cup roasted blue corn, finely ground
1 cup white flour
1 Tablespoon baking powder
1/4 teaspoon salt
8 ounces cream cheese
2 eggs

The Filling:
1/2 cup tomato purée seasoned with garlic, basil, and oregano
2 cups grated cheese (jack, mozzarella, or provolone)

Optional Additions:
small amounts of diced mushrooms , chiles, olives, onions, artichoke hearts

If making a fresh tomato sauce for the filling, start it ahead of time, so it can cool before being used in the pastiche. Tomato purée seasoned with garlic, basil and oregano is my favorite sauce. Feel free to use your own. While the oven preheats to 450°, grate the cheese-or a combination of cheeses, and dice any other additions. (These are great absolutely plain, don't feel compelled to add veggies. To decide what to use, think along the lines of pizza toppings.)

For the dough, combine the blue corn, white flour, and salt. Mix well. Blend the cream cheese into the flour. Now add the two eggs and work the dough (adding small amounts of flour as necessary) to create a soft but not sticky consistency. Pinch off an egg-size ball and roll it out into a circle no more than 1/4 inch thick.

Allowing 3/4 inch between the edge of the dough and the filling, place about a 1/4 cup grated cheese, a Tablespoon of sauce, and various goodies on the circle of dough. Fold the circle in half and seal edges by rolling the dough toward the center of the pie, fold it under, and crimp between the thumb and index finger. Do not poke holes in the crust!

Place the pies on an ungreased baking sheet and bake for 10-12 minutes at 450°.

Makes 8.

CHICKEN BASKETS

This is a truly shocking and delicious meal of green chiles, chicken, and cheese cradled in lavender baskets. It's one of my favorites.

The Filling:
4 pieces bacon, cooked and crumbled
1 onion, diced
1 clove garlic, pressed
2 chicken breasts, into diced 1/2 inch cubes
1 cup green chiles, diced
1/2 cup sharp cheddar cheese, grated
1 teaspoon Dijon mustard
2 Tablespoons sour cream
salt & pepper to taste

The Basket:
1 cup roasted blue corn, finely ground
1 teaspoon baking powder
1 cup sour cream

Preheat the oven to 350°. Sauté the onion, garlic, and diced chicken breasts in a heavy frying pan. In a bowl, combine the chicken mixture with the bacon, chiles, mustard, salt, pepper, and sour cream. Mix well and set aside.

To prepare the baskets, combine the blue corn, baking powder and sour cream. Spoon this mixture into well-seasoned muffin tins. If you don't have well-seasoned pans, you need to grease them with a little oil. Fill 9 cups about half-way. Using a soup spoon, add filling to the center of each muffin cup, forcing the filling into the center and allowing the batter to rise up along the sides. Distribute the filling evenly and then bake for 15 minutes.

Allow to cool slightly before removing form the tins. Loosen the edges with a sharp knife, then use a spoon to lift each basket out. These will come out in perfect baskets if the spoon is placed under the middle to give support in lifting them out.

Serves four to five.

BAKED CHICKEN

This is a simple and unusual twist to the ubiquitous baked chicken. A little cayenne pepper will add a nice kick for the daring.

    1 medium chicken, cut into parts for baking
    2 eggs
    1 cup roasted blue corn, finely ground
    1/2 cup walnuts, finely ground
    1/3 cup parmesan cheese
    1/4 teaspoon salt
    2 Tablespoons dried basil
    cayenne pepper, optional

Mix all of the dry ingredients in one bowl. In a flat bottom bowl, beat the eggs. Remove the skin from chicken parts. Dip the chicken parts into the egg and roll them in dry ingredients. Bake for 35-40 minutes at 350°.
Serves four.

HAYDÉE'S REMARKABLE CHICKEN

True to an impassioned artist's lifestyle, Haydée rarely cooks. She knows one recipe, so I was intrigued when she offered to make it for me. I was quite impressed and adapted her basic recipe to include in this collection. The end result is an unusually spiced chicken in a thick lavender crust.

4 chicken breasts
2 cups sour cream
1 Tablespoon Worcestershire sauce
2 teaspoons paprika
1 teaspoon pepper
1 teaspoon celery salt
juice of 1 lemon
2 pressed garlic cloves
2 cups roasted blue corn, finely ground

Combine the sour cream, Worcestershire sauce, paprika, pepper, celery salt, lemon juice, and garlic. Remove the skin and marinate the chicken overnight in this exotic sour cream mixture. If boneless chicken breast are used, reduce the cooking time by about 12 minutes. Preheat the oven to 350°. Roll the chicken parts in the blue corn and place them on an ungreased baking sheet. Bake for 30-40 minutes.

Serves four.

MEAT-FILLED TURNOVERS

These turnovers can be presented as part of an elegant dinner or simply eaten as sandwiches. They're good hot, cold, and reheated.

The Pastry:
2 cups white flour
2 cups roasted blue corn, finely ground
1 teaspoon salt
1 cup butter
1 egg + 2 Tablespoons milk

The Filling:
1 red or green bell pepper, chopped
1 pound ground beef
1 medium onion, diced
1 clove garlic, minced
1 cup corn, fresh or frozen
1 Tablespoon chile powder, or more according to taste
1 Tablespoon flour
1/2 teaspoon salt
dash of pepper

Sauté the ground beef, onion, garlic, and bell pepper. Add the corn, salt and pepper. In a small cup or glass, combine chile powder and flour; add about 1/4 cup of water to this and mix well. When this mixture is added to the beef, it will create a spicy gravy that will need a little attention. Add small amounts of water as the sauce is absorbed by the meat. If too much water is added, simply wait a few minutes and allow the sauce to cook down (or thicken up-depending on point of view). In the end it is important to achieve a thick sauce which glazes the meat. Preheat the oven to 450°.

Combine the flour, blue corn, and salt. Cut in the butter and add drops of milk to moisten the dough. When there is a smooth workable dough, pull off small pieces (about the size of a small egg) and roll them out on a lightly floured board. These can be made any size, but, at first, aim for a 1/4 inch thick circle about 5 inches wide. Combine the egg and 2 Tablespoons of milk in a cup and beat. Brush the rim of the dough with the egg mixture; place 1 heaping Tablespoon of filling in the center of the circle; fold the circle in half and press the edges with a fork to seal.

Poke a few air holes in top of each turnover and place them on a baking sheet. Bake 10-12 minutes.

Makes about 16 turnovers.

STUFFED SOLE

This is a glorious and very simple entrée. If you have more time and want to have your friends moaning with delight, cover the stuffed sole with a white sauce of your choice just before serving.

> 12 fillets of English Sole
> 1 Tablespoon butter
> 1 bunch scallions, diced
> 1 med. clove garlic, pressed
> 1 1/2 cup Jack cheese, grated
> 1/2 cup sour cream
> 1 egg
> 1 cup blue corn, finely ground
> 1/4 teaspoon cumin
> 1/4 teaspoon dill
> 1/2 teaspoon baking powder

Preheat the oven to 350°. In a small bowl, combine the blue corn, cumin, dill, and baking powder. In a larger bowl, combine the sour cream, egg, and cheese. sauté the diced scallions in butter and add the dry ingredients to the wet and stir well.

Each stuffed sole is in fact made of three fillets, one for the bottom and two for the sides, which gives the appearance of being one very thick fillet sliced open. Select the four largest pieces of sole and place on a lightly greased baking sheet. These will be the base fillets. On each base add a large dollop of filling, about two inches high and as long as the fillet. Do not spread the filling to the edges. Now, as if building a card house, lay two pieces of sole (one for each side) around the filling; they should rest on the base fillet and touch each other at the ends. When all four servings have been completed, go back and add additional filling where appropriate. The filling should hold the two side fillets at least 1 and 1/2 inches apart (the exact size will, of course, depend on the size of the fillets being used.) Bake for about 20 minutes.

Serves four.

PIZZA

This crust is superb for any style of toppings. If you don't already have a favorite, this recipe will launch you in the right direction.

The Crust:
1 cup roasted blue corn, finely ground
1 cup unbleached white flour
1/4 teaspoon salt
2/3 cup milk

The Sauce:
1 large can tomato purée
pinch of basil, thyme, salt, pepper, garlic

The Toppings:
2 3/4 cups provolone, grated
3/4 cup feta cheese, crumbled
tomato, purple onion, green chiles, olives, all thinly sliced

The Accessories:
olive oil
14" pizza pan (a cookie sheet or cast iron skillet of similar size will be fine)

Preheat the oven to 450°. In a small sauce pan, combine the tomato purée and herbs in some savory proportion of your own design. Allow the sauce to simmer and adjust seasoning, if necessary. While the sauce is cooking, prepare the toppings and set aside.

To make the crust, combine the dry ingredients and blend well. In a measuring cup, combine the milk and olive oil. Add the wet ingredients to the dry ingredients and knead until dough is smooth. On a lightly floured surface, roll out the dough to meet the dimensions of the pie pan. Place the dough on the pie pan and work with finger tips to achieve an accurate fit. Since the crust functions as a containment wall for the goodies, it is important to make some embankment (1/4" minimum), but it is not necessary to make a large, bulky rim.

Once the crust is complete, brush it with a few Tablespoons of olive oil.

Next comes the sauce. Coat the entire surface lightly with sauce — this may mean a few sparse patches. If there is too much sauce, the toppings will slide off the finished pizza. After the sauce, apply the toppings evenly. Bake for 20 minutes.

Makes 6 hearty slices.

ENCHILADAS

Some people have expressed anxiety about purchasing packaged blue corn tortillas because they aren't able to tell whether or not the tortillas are moldy. A local grocery store stopped carrying them for just that reason. Sad but true.

Mold on blue corn tortilla starts off looking like a distinct bruise—dark and round. Once you have recognized this, it is easy to distinguish mold from the natural striations of the tortilla (which are linear, not circular). As the mold progresses, it will turn either floury white or green.

Since I have never been able to make blue corn tortillas that are both thin and strong enough to be used for enchiladas, I suggest packaged tortillas for this (and several other) recipes.

The Sauce:
1 small onion, minced
2 Tablespoons oil
1 robust clove of garlic, pressed
2 Tablespoons chile powder (use 1/2 teaspoon increments when adding chile powder the first time you make this recipe)
1 teaspoon cumin (use less cumin if you use less chile powder)

1 Tablespoon cornstarch
1 cup tomato purée
1 3/4 cups chicken broth (reserve 1/4 cup for thickener)

The Enchiladas:
1 package blue corn tortillas
2 cup cheddar or jack cheese, grated
1/2 cup black olives, sliced
3 scallions, chopped

In a medium-sized nonferrous frying pan, sauté the onion and garlic in 2 Tablespoons oil. When onions are translucent, add chile powder and cumin. Stir well, then add tomato puré and 1 and 1/2 cups chicken broth. Mix the reserved 1/4 cup chicken broth with 1 Tablespoon cornstarch. When the cornstarch is well dissolved, add this mixture to the pan. Stir well and allow to simmer over low heat to thicken the sauce. Adjust spices to taste and proceed either with this or another recipe.

Preheat the oven to 350°. Pour a little enchilada sauce over the bottom of an 8" x 8" glass baking dish. Warm the tortillas on a griddle to soften them (if you have trouble folding them, add a little oil to the griddle and lightly fry the tortillas). As the tortillas come off of the griddle, place grated cheese, olives, and scallions in the center of each. Gently roll and place seam-side down in baking dish. Repeat. Pour enchilada sauce over the pan of enchiladas. Cover with additional cheese if desired. Bake for 15 minutes at 350°.

Makes 8 enchiladas.

ITALIAN-STYLE ENCHILADAS

If you're like me, finding the natural divisions between enchiladas under all of the sauce and melted cheese is a real challenge. This may not be your most elegant meal of the month, but it may be among the most delicious.

15 ounces skim ricotta cheese
1/2 cup black olives, diced
1 cup sharp white cheddar, grated
1/2 teaspoon salt
1 egg
1 cup mozzarella, grated
Enchilada Sauce (See recipe page 55)
6-8 blue corn tortillas

Prepare the enchilada sauce. While it simmers, combine the ricotta cheese, egg, cheddar, salt and olives in a medium size bowl. Pour a small amount of sauce in an 8" x 8" pan to barely cover the bottom. Hold a tortilla in one hand and place a large dollop of ricotta down the middle of it. Gently roll the enchiladas and place seam down in the pan. When the pan is full, pour the remaining sauce over the enchiladas and cover with the mozzarella. Bake 15-20 minutes at 350°.

Makes 6-8 very rich enchiladas.

CHAPTER FIVE

Side Dishes

DINAH'S DUMPLIN'S

Unlike dense soup dumplings, Dinah's dumplings are crisp on the outside and cake-like on the inside. With a little butter and syrup, they make an excellent snack on a cool evening.

> 2 cups roasted blue corn, finely ground
> 1/2 teaspoon salt
> boiling water
> oil for frying
> butter, honey, or maple syrup as condiments

Combine the salt and blue corn. Add just enough boiling water to the blue corn to make the dough stiff and manageable, but not dry or sticky. Mix well. Shape the dough into dumplings. The dumplings should be about an inch thick and twice as long to cook evenly.

Deep fry in hot oil (about 1 inch of oil in a frying pan) until golden brown. Serve immediately with butter and maple syrup (or honey).

Makes about 16 dumplings.

BLUE CORN HUSH PUPPIES

Hush puppies are edging French fries off my menu when I serve shrimp, fried clams, or barbecued chicken.

> 1 1/2 cups roasted blue corn, finely ground
> 1/2 cup flour
> 2 teaspoons baking powder
> 1/4 teaspoon salt
> 1 egg
> 3/4 cup milk
> 1 small onion, grated
> fat for deep-frying

Combine the blue corn, flour, baking powder, and salt. In another bowl, combine the egg, milk, and onion. Add the wet ingredients to the dry ingredients and mix well. Carefully drop batter from a spoon into hot fat. When hush puppies are gold and crisp (about one minute), lift from fat, and allow to drain on a paper towel. Serve hot.

Makes about 20.

SPICY BLUE CORN BREAD

This cornbread is hot and gooey. It's a great dish to serve to shy folks; it always gets a conversation going.

1 1/2 cups roasted blue corn, finely ground
1/2 teaspoon salt
1 Tablespoon baking powder
1 cup onion, chopped
1 cup sour cream
1 1/2 cups cheddar cheese, grated
2-4 jalapeño peppers, minced

Combine the blue corn, salt, baking powder, and onion. Add the sour cream and mix well. Pour half of the batter into a well-greased 9" x 9" pan. Sprinkle half of the cheese and all of the peppers over the batter. Cover with remaining cheese and then dollop the remaining batter over all of this. Bake for 20 minutes at 350°, or until a knife inserted to the center comes out clean.
Makes 9-12 slices.

GRANDMA HATTIE'S BLUE CORN BREAD

This is a very light, cake-like bread that disappears very fast. Luckily, it's easy to make more.

> 1 1/2 cups roasted blue corn, finely ground
> 2 teaspoons baking powder
> 3 Teaspoons sugar
> 3/4 cup milk
> 1 large egg
> 3 Tablespoons safflower oil

Blend the dry ingredients together. Next, combine the wet ingredients and add them to the dry. Mix well. Pour into a well-greased 8" x 8" pan. Bake for 30 minutes at 350°.
Makes 9-12 servings.

KATE'S BLUE CORN CAKE

Kate's decadence is sure to become legendary. This recipe will give you a good idea of how she earned her reputation.

> 2 1/2 cups roasted blue corn, finely ground
> 1 1/2 cups whole wheat pastry flour
> 2 teaspoons baking powder
> 2/3 cup maple syrup
> 1/2 cup melted butter
> 1 cup milk
> 4 eggs
> 1 cup half & half

Combine the dry ingredients together. Add the milk and half & half to the dry ingredients. Stir well and then add butter and syrup. Pour into a well-greased 9" x 13" pan and bake for 30-35 minutes at 350°. Makes 24 servings.

TAOS BLUE CORN BREAD

The smell of green chiles cutting through the smoky flavor of this corn bread always evokes crisp fall mornings in Taos for me. The chiles in this recipe can be omitted or increased.

> 1 1/2 cups roasted blue corn, finely ground
> 2 teaspoons baking powder
> 1 Tablespoon sugar
> 3/4 cup milk
> 1 large egg, beaten
> 3 Tablespoons bacon fat (butter can be
>   substituted)
> 1/4 cup green chiles, chopped (fresh, frozen,
>   or canned)

Preheat the oven to 350° and lightly grease an 8" square pan. Combine the dry ingredients. Mix the milk and egg; then add them to the dry ingredients. Stir in the melted bacon fat and mix lightly. Add the chopped green chiles, mix well, and pour into the lightly greased pan. Bake for 30 minutes.

Makes one dozen servings.

CHAPTER SIX

Soups, Stews, and Casseroles

TAMALE PIE

If you peek while this is cooking, don't be disappointed to find that your crust has disappeared into the murky depths. It will resurface. Serve with sour cream and grated cheese for a lively and decadent feast.

The Crust:
3/4 cup roasted blue corn,
  finely ground
2 Tablespoons flour
1/2 teaspoon salt
2 teaspoons baking powder
1 egg
1/4 cup milk
1 Tablespoon butter

The Basic Filling:
1 large onion, diced
1 1/2 pounds ground beef
2 cloves garlic, pressed
2 Tablespoons chile powder
1 Tablespoon flour
1/2 teaspoon salt
dash of pepper
1/4 teaspoon cinnamon

Optional:
1/4 cup of red or green bell pepper,
olives, corn.

Preheat the oven to 425°. sauté the onion, garlic, and any optional ingredients with the ground beef. Add salt and pepper to taste. In a small cup or glass, combine the chile powder and flour; add about 1/4 cup of water to this and mix well. When this mixture is added to the beef, it will thicken. Add small amounts of water as the sauce is absorbed by the meat. If too much water is added, simply wait a few minutes and allow the sauce to thicken. When a thick, gravy-like sauce is achieved, the gravy is ready. Pour into a 2 quart casserole pan or deep iron skillet.

For the Crust:
Combine the dry ingredients in one bowl and mix well. Then mix the egg and milk together; melt the butter and add it to the milk. Slowly combine the wet and dry ingredients. Cover the filling with the blue corn crust mixture. Bake 20-25 minutes.
Serves four to six.

RABBIT STEW

The blue corn in this stew allows the broth to thicken without creating a heavy gravy. If fresh rabbit is unavailable, substitute chicken.

> 1 medium rabbit, deboned
> 2 Tablespoons oil
> 1 large onion, diced
> 1 clove garlic, pressed
> 2 carrots, diced
> 2 quarts water
> 1 Tablespoon chile powder
> 1 teaspoon salt
> 1/2 cup blue corn, finely ground

Dice the rabbit into cubes and sauté in oil with onion, garlic, and carrots until browned. Add the chile powder. Fill a sauce pan with water and add the salt and the rabbit. Simmer for 1 1/2 hours. Add small amounts of broth to the 1/2 cup of blue corn; remove all lumps and continue to add broth until a smooth, thin mixture is obtained; add this to the stew and simmer 10 more minutes, allowing the broth to thicken. Serve with tortillas or cornbread.

Serves four.

TOFU CASSEROLE

Blue corn adapts very well to vegetarian meals and can be worked into favorite recipes in place of whole wheat flour.

3 Tablespoons butter
3 Tablespoons flour
1 1/2 cups milk
1 1/2 Tablespoons red miso or 1 Tablespoon soy
    sauce
1 clove garlic, crushed
dash of pepper
10 ounces tofu, cut into small pieces
1/2 cup grated cheese
1 onion, thinly sliced
1 carrot, grated
1/2 cup roasted blue corn, finely ground

Preheat the oven to 350°. Grease a shallow casserole dish. In a large cast iron frying pan, sauté butter and garlic. Make a roux by adding the flour and then very gradually add the milk. Stir constantly to prevent lumping. Add miso or soy sauce to this mixture. Next, add the cheese, onion, carrot, tofu, and a dash of pepper according to taste. Mix well and pour into the greased casserole dish. Sprinkle blue corn over the top and bake for 20-25 minutes.
Serves four to six.

LAMB SOUP

It's best to make the soup a day ahead of time, so the fat can be skimmed from the top. Just before serving, add the dumplings.

1 medium onion, diced
1 Tablespoon butter
2 cups lamb, diced
1 cup zucchini, diced
1 cup fresh or frozen corn
4 cups water
1 teaspoon salt
1 teaspoon chile powder
blue corn dumplings (see recipe on page 21)

In a large sauce pan, sauté the butter, onion, and lamb. Add zucchini, corn, chile powder, and salt. Add water and simmer for 1 hour. Allow to cool completely. Excess fat will rise to the surface and can be skimmed off to produce a clear, light broth. Reheat and add blue corn dumplings 15 minutes before serving. This will thicken the broth. Adjust the consistency according to your preference by adding more water.

Serves four.

NO ORDINARY BEAN SOUP

I prefer to make soup a day ahead of time and adjust the spices when reheating, to give the flavor more time to ripen. Do not strive to create a thick broth, as the broth will thicken from the dumplings.

3 cups navy beans
1 carrot, diced
2 heads broccoli, cut into pieces
1/2 head cauliflower, cut into pieces
2 teaspoons thyme
1 teaspoon nutmeg
1 clove garlic, crushed
2 teaspoons basil
1 teaspoon oregano
salt to taste
blue corn dumplings (see recipe on page 21)

Cook the beans in a large soup pot with a lot of water. When beans show signs of being done, add the vegetables to the beans. Simmer for 20 more minutes, then add spices. Fifteen minutes before serving, add the dumplings.

Serves six to eight.

TOFU POT PIE

If you're not fond of tofu, try your favorite pie recipe using a blue corn crust. The rich nutty flavor of blue corn will hold its own against a heavy gravy.

1 unbaked blue corn pie crust
(see recipe on page 95)

The Gravy:
1/2 cup nutritional yeast
1/4 cup flour
1/3 cup oil
1 1/2 cups water
2-3 Tablespoons soy sauce
1 Tablespoon Dijon mustard
1/8 teaspoon pepper

The Filling:
1/2 cup roasted blue corn, finely ground
2 Tablespoons nutritional yeast
4 cups tofu, cut into cubes
1 cup onion, chopped
1 cup celery, chopped
1/2 cup carrots, chopped
1 1/4 cups peas

Preheat the oven to 350° and begin the gravy. In a heavy frying pan, combine the flour, yeast, and oil to make a roux. Slowly add water and stir. Add the soy sauce, mustard, and pepper. Cook until this has a thick gravy consistency-add water or allow water to cook off as needed.

Put the blue corn and yeast into a paper or plastic bag. Dredge tofu by adding it to the bag and shaking it to coat the tofu pieces. Then sauté the tofu in oil until brown. Add onions, celery, carrots, and peas. Cook for about 5 minutes. Pour into the unbaked pie shell and cover with gravy. Bake 15-20 minutes at 350°.

Serves four to six.

CHICKEN SOUP WITH BLUE CORN NOODLES

Blue corn noodles are a delicious addition to any version of chicken soup. This one is a favorite of mine.

Soup Stock:
assorted chicken parts (back, wings, thighs, neck)
4 quarts water
2 bay leaves
1 large onion, diced
three ribs of celery, diced (including leaves)
2 carrots, diced
Salt
fresh black pepper
1 teaspoon dill
2 jalapeño chiles, diced
6 sprigs cilantro, chopped
blue corn noodles (1/2 the recipe on page 84)

Fill a large soup pot with water and add the chicken, bay leaves, onion, carrots, and celery. Bring to a boil and simmer 30-45 minutes. Add the salt, pepper, and dill. Simmer 15-20 minutes. Refrigerate the stock overnight before using.

When the stock has been adequately chilled, the fat will rise to the surface and solidify. Discard all fat; remove the chicken parts and separate the meat from the bones and skin. Put the meat back into the broth.

Add jalapeños to the stock (seeds and all). Bring the stock to a boil and add the blue corn noodles. Reduce heat and simmer until noodles are done. Add cilantro and turn off the heat. Allow to stand for a few minutes before serving.

Serves four to six.

MISO SOUP

There are many kinds of miso. Generally, the darkest misos are the saltiest. Brown rice miso is in the mid-range of saltiness. If you find the miso flavor too strong but don't want to thin-out the soup, add extra ginger.

> 4 quarts water
> 2 Tablespoons brown rice miso
> 1 medium onion, sliced
> 2 carrots, thinly sliced
> 1-2 Tablespoons fresh ginger, finely grated
> 2 Tablespoons oil
> Options: blue corn dumplings (page 61) or blue
> corn noodles (1/2 the recipe on page 84)

Heat the water to boil in a large soup pot. In a large frying pan, lightly sauté onions, cabbage and carrots in the oil. If either dumplings or pasta are used in the soup, add them now to the plain, boiling water and cook until done.

Turn the boiling water off. Using a spoon (holding the miso) and fork, add the miso paste to the water by placing the spoon under water and gently rubbing the fork into the miso. This will release the miso into the water without lumping. Never allow the miso to boil as boiling destroys the protein. sauté the vegetables. Add to the water along with the ginger.

Serves four to six.

CHAPTER SEVEN

Pasta

Pasta, for very little work, will elicit admiration from friends and family for a very long time. There is something about homemade pasta that adds an air of capability and authenticity to meals.

Although making blue corn pasta is not the same as making regular pasta, some of the same rules apply: 1. create a well in the dough for adding wet ingredients; 2. never add dry ingredients directly to the dough; 3. knead the dough without mercy; 4. add as little "extra" flour as possible. Because flours and climates vary, you will not be able to idly follow any pasta recipe; however, you will have all the information you need to make adjustments if your dough is not immediately perfect.

These are virtually fool-proof pasta recipes. Throughout the recipes, you will see notes about what to do when something goes wrong. This does not mean that the recipes are difficult, only that it is next to impossible to ruin them.

Once you have assembled the necessary ingredients and tools, you should plan to spend about an hour actually making pasta (and filling) for the first time.

Equipment

Do not buy a pasta machine. If you own one and want to use it, have at it. I began making pasta by hand at age eight and have continued in my archaic ways ever since. If you plan to make ravioli, do buy a ravioli press. It's a wonderful, simple, and inexpensive tool. I find the press to be indispensable. It is the length and width of an egg carton with holes for a dozen ravioli. There are only two pieces to this press: a metal bottom, which has holes and sculpted edges, and a plastic top which contains little egg-like indentations that fit into the holes to press the dough into cup shapes.

The last piece of equipment (outside of the usual baking pans, utensils and so forth) is a rolling pin. Much to my surprise, I have seen very fine kitchens that do not have a rolling pin. If yours is one of them, then you must also know that a long jar will serve the purpose. If you are using a jar, fill it with beans (the extra weight will help). However, if you plan to make pasta with any regularity, it is necessary to have a rolling pin.

Pasta, for very little work, will elicit admiration from friends and family for a very long time. There is something about homemade pasta that adds magic to meals.

Although making blue corn pasta is not the same as making regular pasta, some of the same rules apply: 1. create a well in the dough for adding wet ingredients; 2. never add dry ingredients directly to the dough; 3. knead the dough without mercy; 4. add as little "extra" flour as possible. Because flours and climates vary, you will not be able to idly follow any pasta recipe; however, you will have all the information you need to make adjustments if your dough is not immediately perfect.

These are virtually fool-proof pasta recipes. Throughout the recipes, you will see notes about what to do when something goes wrong. This does not mean that the recipes are difficult, only that it is next to impossible to ruin them. There is always a way to fix a problem, although the solutions are not always intuitive.

Once you have assembled the necessary ingredients and tools, you should plan to spend about an hour actually making pasta (and filling) for the first time.

Equipment

Do not buy a pasta machine. If you own one and want to use it, have at it. I began making pasta by hand at age eight and have continued in my archaic ways ever since. If you plan to make ravioli, do buy a ravioli press. It's a wonderful, simple, and inexpensive tool. I find the press to be indispensable. It is the length and width of an egg carton with holes for a dozen ravioli. There are only two pieces to this press: a metal bottom, which has holes and sculpted edges, and a plastic top which contains little egg-like indentations that fit into the holes to press the dough into cup shapes.

The last piece of equipment (outside of the usual baking pans, utensils and so forth) is a rolling pin. Much to my surprise, I have seen very fine kitchens that do not have a rolling pin. If yours is one of them, then you must also know that a long jar will serve the purpose. If you are using a jar, fill it with beans (the extra weight will help). However, if you plan to make pasta with any regularity, it is well worth having a rolling pin.

Ingredients

You will need the finest grind of roasted blue corn possible and semolina flour. Semolina can be purchased at health food and gourmet stores. Semolina appears to be very granular, but as you will see, it soon becomes quite gummy and will be the substance that holds everything together, enabling the dough to stretch. Do not try to make blue corn pasta with standard wheat flour. Common wheat flour (whole, bleached or unbleached) contains gluten, a type of protein that enables the dough to stretch. This is the reason why it works so well when combined with blue corn for breads and cakes. Blue corn pasta, however, requires a flour with even more stretch than regular gluten can provide. You may find two varieties of semolina: whole wheat durham semolina and processed semolina (sometimes called durham semolina; durham is the name of the wheat). I prefer to use processed semolina over the whole wheat semolina when combining it with blue corn.

Next, you need salt, eggs, and olive oil. If you do not already have a strong preference for olive oils, or an open bottle in your cabinet, buy a light colored, cold-pressed olive oil. Do not waste your money on the highly processed olive oils advertised as extra light; you'd be trading good olive oil for a good advertising campaign.

BLUE CORN RAVIOLI

When you begin this recipe, you should have a thick wonderful pot of tomato sauce simmering its way to perfection on the stove or stored in the refrigerator.

1 cup roasted blue corn, fine ground
1 cup semolina
1 teaspoon salt

2 medium eggs
3 Tablespoons olive oil
white flour

Measure out the dry ingredients. Don't shake down the measuring cup when measuring the flours. Evenly mix the blue corn, semolina, and salt in a large mixing bowl. Dig a small hole (called a well) in the middle of the mixture. Fill the well with two unbeaten eggs and 3 Tablespoons of olive oil. Using a fork, whip the egg and oil mixture, gradually picking up the surrounding flour in each stroke. When a ball of dough forms, knead the remaining flour into the ball. At this point you must assess the dough. If the dough is tacky but does not stick to your hands, congratulations. Using a lightly floured surface (white flour), knead the ball of dough about twelve minutes. The color will change from a dull steel to a beautiful blue as the dough becomes smooth and satiny. Consider yourself a success and skip the next three paragraphs.

If the dough cracks and crumbles, wet your hands well, and knead dough again. This is the only acceptable way of adding water to the dough. You may do this twice. If you can't get a satiny shine to your dough after kneading it for several minutes, it must have been drier than you first suspected. Remember this for the future and go on to the next paragraph.

If too much flour was used or the eggs were too small, the dough will be dry and clumpy. In this case, you will need to add one more egg. This is preferable to losing the dough, but should be done only as a last resort. Be sure it is well beaten before adding it to the dough. It will require hands-on squishing to get the egg to blend evenly. Now the dough will be too wet to knead, so allow it to rest for about ten minutes. The flours will absorb the extra moisture. While the dough is resting, clean your work area and prepare the filling. Now, on a lightly floured board, begin to knead the dough. It is okay if the dough is still tacky. It will pick up enough white flour from the board to remedy this.

The last possibility is that a remarkable hen left you very large eggs and now, after only using two eggs, the dough is too wet to knead. Allow the dough to rest and proceed as suggested in the previous paragraph.

RAVIOLI FILLING

15 ounces skim ricotta cheese
2 eggs
1/2 cup parsley, minced
1/2 cup parmesan, grated

2 Tablespoons butter, melted
a pinch of basil
a dash of pepper

Combine all ingredients in a large mixing bowl and stir well. Adjust seasonings. Fill a large pot with lightly salted water and bring it to a low boil. Pull off a fist of dough, and, on a smooth surface (if the surface is hard and smooth, it will not need to be floured), roll out a rectangle of dough slightly larger than the ravioli press and as thin as possible.

Lay this piece of dough lightly over the bottom of the press. Gently place the top of the press on the dough and ease it into place, forcing the dough to bulge through the holes. If the dough tore at the center of more than two ravioli, it is a sign that the dough is too thin. If the dough tore at the edges of the press, where the ravioli begins to push out, then the dough is too thick. In either case, pull up all of the dough and start again.

It is okay if a few of the ravioli tear now and then. Unlike traditional ravioli, these tears will seal when the ravioli cooks.

Use a teaspoon to fill each ravioli to the brim. Do not overfill. Excess filling in ravioli will force its way between the top and bottom layers and cause the ravioli to break open. Too little filling will cause the tops of the ravioli to pucker with craters.

Roll out a very thin rectangle of dough to be placed over the ravioli tray. Smooth the dough over the tray, and, with a rolling pin, firmly and gently roll over the tray, forcing the ravioli to seal as the sculpted edges of the frame rise to the surface. Pull away excess dough and then remove each ravioli from the tray by gently tugging at its edges.

To cook, drop 6-8 ravioli into boiling water. If the water is not at a low boil, the ravioli will sink and stick to the bottom of the pot. If the water is at a fast boil, you will risk tearing the ravioli apart. It will take about three minutes for the ravioli to surface from the bottom. Skim them out with a slotted spoon. Serve covered with tomato sauce and grated cheese. If preferred, cover the bottom of a baking dish with tomato sauce and layer raviolis, sauce, and grated cheese.

Prepared in a baking dish, ravioli can then be refrigerated for a day or even frozen. To serve, bake at 350° for fifteen minutes.

Makes 3 dozen.

SPANISH-STYLE RAVIOLI

If you enjoy Southwestern cooking, you've just found heaven with this recipe.

> 1 cup skim ricotta
> 2 eggs
> 1 cup diced chiles (New Mexican or Anaheim
>   peppers fresh, frozen, or canned)
> 1/2 cup sharp cheddar cheese, grated
> 1/4 teaspoon sage
> 2 Tablespoons butter, melted
> dash of salt and pepper

First prepare the enchilada sauce on page 56. Next, prepare pasta for ravioli on page 81 and follow the same guidelines for assembly, using this filling instead of the traditional and substituting enchilada sauce for tomato sauce.

If fresh chiles are used, obviously, they must be roasted and skinned (seeding is optional) before being diced.

Makes 3 dozen.

BLUE CORN EGG NOODLES

I learned the meaning of thin from my mother. We would roll out egg noodles on the kitchen table and then either hang them to dry on a broom handle suspended between chairs or nest them in clusters on the counters. She insisted that the dough be thin enough to read through. I was just learning to read and this idea appealed to me, despite the blisters.

I realize that this idea may not now appeal to you, but fortunately, a very small amount of dough will make enough noodles for a large pot of soup.

    1 cup roasted blue corn, finely ground
    1 cup semolina
    1 teaspoon salt
    3 eggs
    3 Tablespoons olive oil

This is a very pliable dough, and it is extremely easy to roll out sheer sheets of dough. Because blue corn is dense and will swell when cooked, these noodles must be so thin that to go any thinner will cause them to fall apart.

Roll out small batches on a cutting board and then use a very sharp knife to cut the pasta into 1/2 inch noodles. Dust a large flat surface (eg., kitchen table) with cornstarch or white flour and then place the noodles, scrunched into small clusters, on the table to dry.

Half of this recipe will provide enough noodles for a huge pot of soup. The other noodles can be frozen for later use. Freeze the dried noodles, not the dough.

CHAPTER EIGHT

Desserts

VANESSA'S HEAVEN

Vanessa is one of the best and most critical cooks I have ever met. Over a period of several years, she withstood innumerable blue corn experiments concocted by Jeanne and me. Her unrestrained enthusiasm for this particular recipe was proof to me that anyone could enjoy blue corn.

The Cake:
1 cup soft unsalted butter
1 cup light brown sugar
4 large eggs
1 cup milk
2 teaspoons vanilla
1 1/2 cups roasted blue corn, finely
   ground
1 1/2 cups unbleached white flour
2 Tablespoons baking powder
1/2 teaspoon salt

The filling:
2/3 cup chocolate chips
2/3 cup walnuts, well-chopped
2/3 cup apricot or peach jam
1/2 cup diced dried peaches or apricots, optional*

*other possible fillings are cinnamon, coconut, almonds, or dried cherries.

Preheat the oven to 350° and grease a bundt pan. If you want the cake to be blue, green or aqua, you'll have to be quick about getting it into the oven once the blue corn is added. But don't worry, this recipe is delicious regardless of color. Measure the filling ingredients, combine the nuts and chocolate in one bowl, but keep the jam and dried fruit separate.

Cream the butter and sugar together. Add the eggs and beat well with an electric mixer. Add the vanilla. Add the milk, taking care that it is mixed in well. If unsalted butter was not used, do not add salt. If you used unsalted butter in the recipe, now is the time to add salt; also add baking powder and white flour. When everything is mixed well, add the blue corn.

Pour 1/2 of the batter into the bundt pan. Place teaspoon-size dollops of jam on top of the batter. Keep the dollops close together and far from the edges. Don't try to spread the jam. Continue adding jam until a solid ring is formed. Now sprinkle the nut and chocolate mixture over the jam, avoiding the sides but making about a 3-inch pathway around the pan. Add the remaining batter by even dollops. Do not try to spread the batter. If you are agile, the batter will be blue-green. Pop it in the oven for about 40 minutes. Test with a cake tester. Let cool for five minutes before turning out onto a cooling rack.

Serves ten.

JEANNE'S BLUE CORN POPPYSEED CAKE

This recipe is yet more proof of Jeanne's genius with blue corn. She is able to combine the right textures, colors, and flavors to make ordinary food extraordinary.

> 1/4 cup unsalted butter
> 1/2 cup plus 2 Tablespoons honey
> 3 eggs
> 1 cup sour cream
> 1 1/2 teaspoons vanilla
> 3/4 cup roasted blue corn
> 1/2 cup whole wheat pastry flour
> 2 Tablespoons powdered milk
> 1/2 cup poppyseed
> 1/2 teaspoon salt

Preheat the oven to 350°. Melt the butter. Then, combine all the wet ingredients, including the butter, in one bowl. In another bowl, combine all the dry ingredients. Blend the dry and wet mixtures. Pour batter into a well-greased bundt pan and bake for 30 minutes at 350°.

Makes 10-12 slices.

BLUE CORN POPPYSEED COOKIES

These are easy to make and are great holiday cookies. An extra plus is that the dough is easy enough for children to handle.

1/2 cup butter
3/4 cup light brown sugar
2 eggs, well beaten
1/2 teaspoon vanilla
1/3 cup poppyseed
1 cup unbleached white flour
1 cup roasted blue corn, finely ground
2 teaspoons baking powder
1/4 teaspoon salt

Cream the butter and sugar together. Add eggs, vanilla, baking powder, and salt. Stir well. Add blue corn and flour and mix well. Add poppyseeds. Chill the dough for an hour. Then on a lightly floured surface, roll out the dough to a 1/4" thickness. Cut into shapes with jars or cookie cutters, place on a cookie sheet, and bake 10-12 minutes at 375°.

Makes about 2 dozen cookies.

BLUE CORN THUMBPRINT COOKIES

This recipe is my all time favorite. It's a variation on one of my mother's recipes. Even when I quadruple the ingredients, it never makes enough!

1/2 cup butter
1/4 cup brown sugar
1 egg yolk (save white for later)
1/2 teaspoon vanilla
1/2 cup roasted blue corn, finely ground
1/2 cup unbleached white flour
1/4 teaspoon salt
3/4 cup walnuts, finely chopped
jam or frosting for the centers

Cream the butter and brown sugar. Add the egg yolk, vanilla, and salt. Mix well. Then, add the blue corn and flour. The dough should be stiff enough to shape into 1" balls. Dip each ball into the egg white and then roll in the finely chopped nuts, coating thoroughly. Place cookies on an ungreased cookie sheet and make a deep imprint with your thumb into each cookie. Bake 10 minutes at 350°. When cooled, fill the center with jam or frosting.

Makes 1 dozen cookies.

BROWNIES

Oat flour will make a chewier, moister brownie. Unbleached white flour can also be used.

> 1/2 cup butter
> 4 ounces, semi-sweet chocolate
> 4 eggs, at room temperature
> 1 cup sugar
> 1 teaspoon vanilla
> 1/2 cup roasted blue corn, finely ground
> 1/2 cup oat flour
> 1 cup walnuts, chopped

Preheat the oven to 350° and grease a 9" x 9" pan. Then, melt the butter and chocolate together in a double boiler or heavy sauce pan. While the chocolate is melting, mix the eggs and sugar together in a bowl. Add the melted chocolate and butter to the sugar and eggs and mix. Then add the vanilla. Slowly add the blue corn and oat flours. Add nuts to the batter last, when all lumps are removed. Pour into the baking pan and bake for 12-15 minutes. Do not overcook.

Makes 9-12 servings.

SHORTBREAD BLUES

Don't be surprised if the shortbread turns out pink! If you feel an odd desire to press this into a tart pan, don't hesitate. This makes an excellent tart crust.

>1 1/2 cups unsalted butter, softened
>2 1/2 cups roasted blue corn, finely ground
>2/3 cup powdered sugar

Mix the sugar and blue corn together; then cream the butter into the mixture. If necessary, sprinkle a few drops of cold water over the dough to make it hold together. Press the batter into a pan, so it is about 1/2" thick. A small cookie sheet works well (score the dough for cookies before baking). Bake 5-10 minutes at 350°.

Makes about 12 servings.

BLUE CORN LAYER CAKE

This cake is a show stopper when it is covered with a chocolate glaze or decorated with fresh fruit (berries, peaches or cherries). The tastiest frostings for a blue corn cake are chocolate and coconut (they enhance both the flavor and the color of the cake).

1/2 cup plus 2 Tablespoons salted butter
2/3 cup sugar
2/3 cup milk
2 eggs
1 teaspoon vanilla
1 cup roasted blue corn, finely ground
1 cup flour
2 teaspoons baking powder
1 teaspoon baking soda

Preheat the oven to 350° and grease two 8" cake pans or one 9 x 13". Cream the butter and sugar together, then add vanilla and eggs. In a separate bowl, combine all the dry ingredients. Slowly add a small portion of the dry ingredients to the butter and stir. Alternately add a little milk, then more of the dry ingredients to keep the batter creamy. Pour immediately into cake pans and bake 15-20 minutes.

An 8" double-layer cake yields about 8 servings; a one-layer 9" x 13" cake yields about 20 servings.

BLUE CORN PIE CRUST

This crust is wonderful for cheesecake or fruit pies; it has to be one of the world's nuttiest, most flavorful crusts! The quantity of butter in this recipe will make it virtually impossible to achieve anything but a conventional brown color, but it's worth it. You will know that it's blue corn the moment you taste it.

     1 cup roasted blue corn, finely ground
     1 cup unbleached white flour
     1 cup salted butter
     ice water

Combine the blue corn and flour and cut in the butter. Gradually add about 2 Tablespoons of ice water to work the batter into a smooth dough. Don't over-work or allow the butter to melt. Wrap in wax paper and chill in the fridge or freezer for one hour or twenty minutes respectively.

Break the dough into two equal sections and roll it out on a well-floured surface to fit a pie pan. This recipe will make a generous top and bottom crust for a 9" pie. Bake at 425° for fifteen minutes for a shell or according to directions for a particular pie filling.

BLUE CORN CHOCOLATE CHIP COOKIES

After turquoise chocolate chip cookies, everything else looks so dull!

> 1 egg
> 1/2 cup sweet butter
> 1/3 cup light brown sugar
> 1 teaspoon vanilla
> 1/2 cup roasted blue corn, finely ground
> 1/2 cup unbleached white flour or oat flour
> 2/3 cup chocolate chips
> walnuts, optional

Cream the butter and sugar together, then add the vanilla and egg. Now add the blue corn and flour and chocolate chips. Add walnuts, if desired. Bake 8-10 minutes at 350°.
Makes 1 dozen cookies.

WALNUT BISCUITS

These heavenly blue biscuits are wonderful with a cup of tea.

> 1/3 cup salted butter
> 2 Tablespoons honey
> 1 egg
> 1/2 cup unbleached white flour
> 3/4 cup roasted blue corn
> 1/2 cup chopped walnuts
> 1 teaspoon baking powder
> 1 teaspoon vanilla

Preheat oven to 350°. Cream the butter, honey, and vanilla together. Add the egg and stir well. In a separate bowl, combine the blue corn, flour, and baking powder together and blend well. Then add the dry ingredients to the butter mixture. Add walnuts.

Pat out dough or use a rolling pin to create biscuits about 2-3 inches wide and 1/2 inch thick. Place on a lightly greased cookie sheet. Allow to stand a few minutes until a soft blue comes through the dough (this is for appearance only; they make beautiful sky-blue mounds). Bake 5-10 minutes.

If preferred, substitute almonds for walnuts and almond extract for the vanilla.

Makes 1 dozen biscuits.

BLUE GENOISE

This is a beautiful, blue cake. It's very light, so don't be embarrassed if you eat the whole thing yourself. It's best fresh and will dry out quickly if left overnight.

> 6 large eggs
> 1 cup sugar
> 1/2 cup roasted blue corn, finely ground
> 1/2 cup flour
> 1/2 cup sweet butter, melted
> 1 teaspoon vanilla

Sift the blue corn and flour together. Heat the eggs and sugar together in a double boiler. As the mixture heats, whip it with a high-speed electric mixer until frothy and thick. Alternately add butter and the mixed blue corn and flour to the eggs, whipping continuously. Add the vanilla. Pour into a greased 8" pan and bake at 350° for 15 minutes until done.

Makes 6 servings.

BLUE CORN BARS

These exotic bars combine the elegance and richness of all my favorite cookies. A thick, dense layer of semi-sweet chocolate covers a shortbread-like pastry.

> 1 cup butter
> 1 cup brown sugar
> 2 teaspoons vanilla
> 2 eggs
> 2 cups oatmeal
> 1 cup roasted blue corn, finely ground
> 1 cup unbleached white flour
> 1 cup semi-sweet chocolate chips
> 2 Tablespoons butter
> 3 Tablespoons water

Preheat the oven to 350°. Cream the butter and sugar together, then add the vanilla and eggs. Stir in the oatmeal, blue corn, and the unbleached white flour. Mix well between each addition. Spread into a 13" x 9" pan and bake for 15 minutes. Cool.

In a double boiler, combine the chocolate, water, and butter. Melt and stir well. Pour the chocolate over the cooled pan of bars-to-be. Let the chocolate harden slightly then cut into bars and refrigerate. (The chocolate will fracture if you try to slice the bars after it has been refrigerated).

Makes 2 dozen servings.

Blue Corn Suppliers

Blue Corn Trading Company
P.O. Box 957
Taos, NM 87571

Casados Farms
P.O. Box 1269
San Juan Pueblo, NM 87566

Native Seeds/SEARCH
2509 N. Campbell Avenue #325
Tucson, AZ 85719

Old Southwest Trading Company
P.O. Box 7545
Albuquerque, NM 87194

Great Southwest Cuisine Catalog
Santa Fe, NM

Pecos Valley Spice Co.
1450 Heggen Street
Hudson, WI 54016

G.B. Ratto and Co.
821 Washington Street
Oakland, CA 94607
800/325-3483

INDEX

Please send me _____ copies of **The Blue Corn Cookbook** for $7.95 each

Name _____ ☐ Payment Enclosed

☐ Bill Me

Address_____

☐ VISAMC

City _____ ☐ American Express

State _____ Zip _____ 1-800-359-1483

Exp. Date_____

Send to: Chile Pepper, P.O. Box 4278
Albuquerque, NM 87196

Please send me _____ copies of **The Blue Corn Cookbook** for $7.95 each

Name _____ ☐ Payment Enclosed

☐ Bill Me

Address_____

☐ VISAMC

City _____ ☐ American Express

State _____ Zip _____ 1-800-359-1483

Exp. Date_____

Send to: Chile Pepper, P.O. Box 4278
Albuquerque, NM 87196

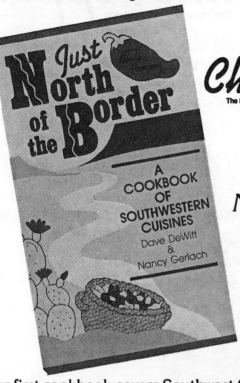